BADGERS

A TRUE BOOK

by

Joan Kalbacken

Children's Press®
A Division of Grolier Publishing
New York London Hong Kong Sydney
Danbury, Connecticut

Reading Consultant
Linda Cornwell
*Learning Resource Consultant
Indiana Department of
Education*

A badger on the prairie

Library of Congress Cataloging-in-Publication Data

Kalbacken, Joan.
    Badgers / by Joan Kalbacken.
        p.   cm. — (A True book)
    Includes bibliographical references and index.
    Summary: Describes the physical characteristics and habits of
these nocturnal mammals, the largest numbers of which are found
in the prairies of western United States and Canada.
    ISBN 0-516-20157-3 (lib.bdg.)   ISBN 0-516-26093-6 (pbk.)
    1. Badgers—Juvenile literature. [1. Badgers.] I. Title. II. Series.
QL737.C25K325 1996
599.74'447—dc20   96-14032
                                                                    CIP
                                                                       AC

Contents

What Are Badgers?

The badger is a mammal about the size of a raccoon. It has a black and gray face marked with white stripes. These short-legged furry animals are found in North America, Europe, and Asia.

There are eight different species of badgers. The

largest numbers of badgers live in the prairies of the western two-thirds of the United States and Canada. According to some scientists, the badger was

A badger on the prairie

American badgers have dark faces with white stripes.

given its name because its facial marks look like a badge. The white stripes may be a badge of warning for the badger's enemies.

A mink

A weasel

A wolverine

An otter

A skunk

Weasels, minks, skunks, wolverines, and otters are relatives of the badger.

Badger Relatives

Badgers belong to the *Mustelidae* family. The word *mustela* is the Latin name for weasel. Weasels, skunks, minks, ferrets, martens, otters, wolverines, and polecats are all members of this family. Animals in the *Mustelidae* family are all *carnivores* (meat eaters). They all have short legs and scent glands. The scent glands release a bad odor when the animal is afraid or angry.

Scientists think the ancestors of the badger came from Southeast Asia nearly 40 million years ago. They also believe that the North American badger may have come across the Bering land strip from Siberia five million years ago.

What do Badgers Eat?

Badgers are *carnivores*, or meat-eaters. The most common badger foods are gophers, rats, mice, prairie dogs, and ground squirrels.

Badgers also eat the larvae of many insects, including bees, wasps, and ants. Water holes provide frogs, crayfish,

A badger with a ground squirrel in its mouth

and minnows for food. Sometimes badgers find birds' eggs on the ground, or young birds that cannot fly. Favorite foods of the western badger include lizards, and even snakes.

Badgers are good at avoiding the bites of poisonous reptiles. With its strong jaws, the badger catches a poisonous snake behind the snake's head. The badger's thick fur protects it from many stings and bites.

A badger facing down a snake

Great Burrowers

Their flat bodies, big claws, and powerful shoulders make badgers very good fighters. They are known for their ability to dig and burrow. They dig burrows very quickly.

The badger has a special inner eyelid that helps it see while working in loose sand

Badgers have long, sharp claws.

and dust. It has big webbed forepaws that it uses like sharp shovels to move the dirt. The bottoms of its forepaws are especially

Badgers aren't bothered by the dirt and sand that fly about as they dig a burrow.

Badgers have a keen sense of smell.

sensitive. Badgers know if roots or stones are in a digging path. They have a keen sense of smell. Their noses warn them of danger.

Badgers like to dig their burrows in loose, sandy soil.

The Badger's Home

A badger home is an under-ground burrow, or tunnel.

Badgers prefer to dig their burrows in soil that is loose and sandy. But they also can dig in very hard, compact soil. They have five toes with sharp claws on each webbed foot. Their claws are longer than a man's fingers.

The entrance of a badger burrow

The burrows are sometimes very deep and long. They keep the badgers warm in cold winters and cool in summer heat. The entrances to the burrows are large, foot-wide holes with mounds of loose dirt near them. Sometimes horses or cattle stumble into the large holes and sprain or break their legs.

Badger burrows have side tunnels off the main tunnel. These are used when they eat or when they feed their young. The badgers are quite safe in their underground homes. They keep the burrows very clean.

Badgers also keep their bodies clean. With their hind feet, they scratch and comb their fur. They lick their fur to keep it clean and shiny.

Badgers inside a burrow

Daily Life

Badgers are nocturnal animals. This means that they are most active at night. Nighttime is when they do their hunting. They listen carefully and sniff for rodents living in the ground. When they find their prey, they quickly dig a tunnel directly into the home of the rodent.

A badger sniffing for rodents

Badgers have very sharp teeth.

With their strong jaws and 34 sharp teeth, they catch and quickly eat the small animal inside its tunnel. A badger eats at least one small rodent every day.

A sleeping badger

During the day, badgers spend most of their time in their dens or burrows. They nap or groom themselves. In rainy or snowy weather, they plug up the entrance to their burrows from the inside. This protects them from cold rain

Badger Families

Most species of badgers like to live alone. They are not very friendly toward one another. However, a pair of badgers will mate in the middle of summer. North American badgers have a new mate each year. The baby badger doesn't begin to

or snow. They sleep through bad-weather days. But they do not hibernate or sleep the entire winter like some mammals do.

Badgers are active in the winter. They do not hibernate, as some mammals do.

A badger mother lying in her den with her month-old cubs

form in the mother's womb
until the winter.

The young are born in the
spring. The mother usually
has two or three babies at a
time. The babies are called

When badger cubs are a few months old, they begin to venture out of the den.

"cubs." Cubs are born blind and have very little fur on their bodies. They are between 3 and 5 inches (7.5 and 12.5 centimeters) long and weigh about 3 ounces (84 grams) at birth.

Mother badgers are called "sows." Like other mammals, they nurse their young. A special side tunnel of the burrow is used for nursing.

After three or four weeks, the cubs are old enough

to eat solid food. The sows bring fresh meat into the den for their babies. The fathers, or "boars," do not help at all with their cubs.

By June, the badger cubs follow their mother out of the burrow to hunt with her. She teaches them to hunt and how to survive by themselves. In a short time, usually a month or two, the young animals go off to dig their own dens and find their own hunting areas.

Badgers and Coyotes

Coyotes and badgers are not really friends. But coyotes like to be near badgers. In the western part of the United States, they are hunting partners. The coyote knows the badger can find the tunnels of ground squirrels and prairie dogs. The coyote crouches at one opening of the rodent's tunnel. When the badger digs into the rodent's home, the coyote pounces on the victim as it leaves the other end of the burrow. The Aztec Indians

Coyotes wait near a badger den.

Dachshunds

Hundreds of years ago, some Germans hunted badgers. They raised special dogs to help them hunt. The small, long dogs could follow the badger into its burrow. The dog's sharp bark would scare the badger out of its hole. This hunting dog was named *dachshund*, a German word that means "badger dog."

call the badger a *talcoyote*, the "coyote of the earth." Badgers do not like coyotes. They steal the badgers' prey.

Badgers scare off predators by hissing and showing their teeth.

Badger Predators

Eagles, ravens, and large coyotes have been known to take small badger cubs. No other species will prey on full-grown badgers. Most animals sense the great fighting power of the badgers. Badgers drive off most predators by hissing, snarling, and showing their sharp teeth.

Badgers are shy but become very angry if cornered. When angry, they raise their short tails and show their sharp teeth. They release a bad odor from special scent glands. A threatened badger faces its enemy and backs slowly into its burrow. If the badger is not near its burrow, it still does not flee. It cannot run very fast. Instead of running, it starts to dig furiously. It shovels the dirt into the face of its attacker.

The badger's strong feet and claws keep its enemy from pulling it out of the hole it is digging.

Automobiles and other highway vehicles are the greatest threat to badgers. The slow-moving badgers are not afraid of cars, trucks, or trains. Badgers are often killed on roads in the western United States.

The

Badger

State

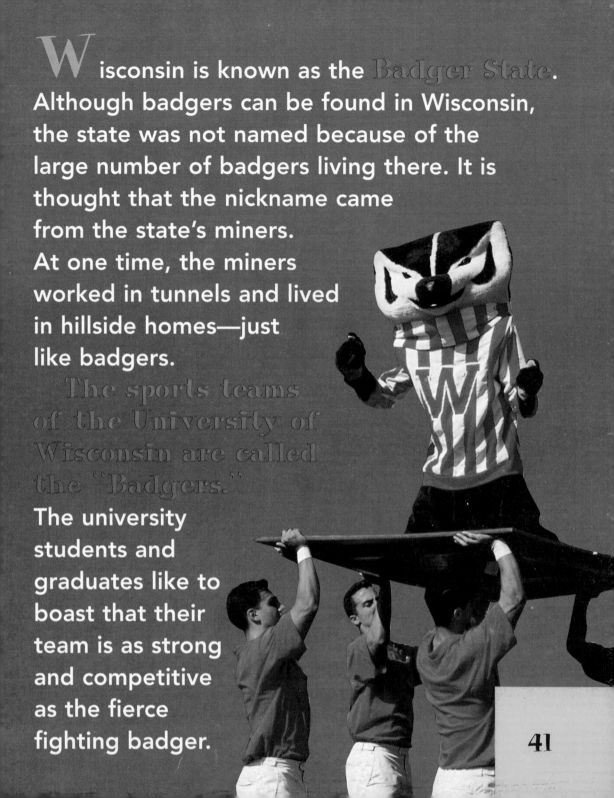

Wisconsin is known as the Badger State. Although badgers can be found in Wisconsin, the state was not named because of the large number of badgers living there. It is thought that the nickname came from the state's miners. At one time, the miners worked in tunnels and lived in hillside homes—just like badgers.

The sports teams of the University of Wisconsin are called the "Badgers."

The university students and graduates like to boast that their team is as strong and competitive as the fierce fighting badger.

41

Badgers of Tomorrow

Because badgers are nocturnal animals, you may not see them except in a zoo. But the badger population is increasing. Badgers have taken advantage of the big parks and recreation areas of the western prairies of the nation. While prairie dogs and

Badgers are fierce little fighters.

ground squirrels are growing in numbers, the badgers will have plenty of food. These amazing little fighters will survive and continue to challenge any predators.

To Find Out More

Here are some additional resources to help you learn more about badgers:

 **Books**

 **Organizations**

Banks, Martin, **Discovering Badgers.** Bookwright Press, 1988.

Bartram, Alan, **Badgers.** Priory Press Ltd, 1974.

Burn, Barbara, **North American Mammals.** Gramercy Books, 1984.

Lavine, Sigmund A., **The Wonders of Badgers.** Dodd, Mead, 1985.

The Mammal Society
15 Cloisters
Business Centre
8 Battersea Park Road,
London, England,
SW8 4 BG
0171 498 4358
0171 498 4459 (fax)

National Park Service
Office of Public Inquiries
P.O. Box 37127
Washington, DC 20013
202-2-8-4747

**Smithsonian: National
Zoological Park**
3000 Block of
Connecticut Avenue, NW
Washington, DC 20008
202-673-4800
*http://www.si.sgi.com/
perspect.afafam/
afazoo.htm*

**American Zoo and
Aquarium Association**
7970-D Old Georgetown Rd.
Bethesda, MD 20814-2493
301-907-7777
301-907-2980 (fax)

**Wildlife Conservation
International**
185th Street
  and Southern Boulevard
New York, NY 10460-1099
212-220-5155
212-220-7114 (fax)

Online Sites

Electronic Zoo
*http://www.zi.biologie.
uni-muenchen.de/
~st2042/ exotic.html*

Friends of the Earth
*http://essential.org/orgs/
FOE/FOE.html*

The Mammal Society
*http://www.abdn.ac.uk/
~nhi600/mammsoc/
mammsoc.html*

**National Parks
Electronic Bookstore**
*http://mesaverde.org/
npeb/books/
10307240584.html*

Weasel Tracks
*http://informns.k12.mn.us/
~moen/february/
WeaselTracks.html*

Important Words

ancestor an animal of an earlier type from which later animals developed

burrower an animal that makes its home by digging a hole in the soil; this home is called a burrow

compact closely and firmly put together

competitive striving for something wanted by others

hibernate to pass the winter in a resting state

larva an insect in its early stage as a caterpillar, grub, or maggot, between hatching from an egg and becoming a pupa

mammal any animal that is warm-blooded, has a backbone, feeds its young with milk, and is covered with hair or fur

prairie a large area of flat, grassy land with few or no trees

predator an animal that hunts another animal

species a group of living things that are more or less alike and whose members can interbreed

Index

Meet the Author

Joan Formell Kalbacken earned a B.A. in Education from the University of Wisconsin, Madison, and an M.A. from Illinois State University. She has been a secondary-school teacher in Beloit, Wisconsin, and Pekin and Normal, Illinois.